DAYS OF CHANGE

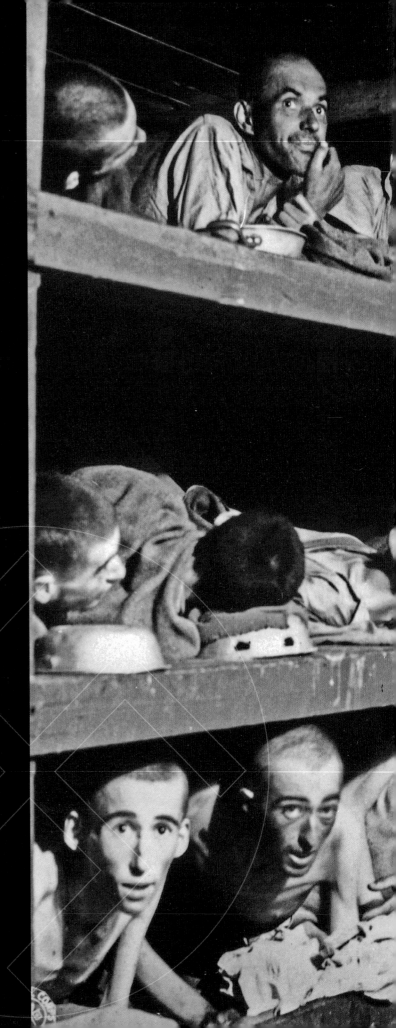

Creative Education

BY VALERIE BODDEN

Published by Creative Education
P.O. Box 227, Mankato, Minnesota 56002
Creative Education is an imprint of The Creative Company.

Cover design and art direction by Rita Marshall
Interior design and book production by The Design Lab
Printed in the United States of America

Photographs by Alamy (Mary Evans Picture Library, POPPER-
FOTO, TIM GRAHAM, Michael Ventura), Corbis (Bettmann,
dpa, Hulton-Deutsch Collection, Yevgeny Khaldei), Getty
Images (Horce Abahams, Hulton Archive, Imagno / Austrian
Archives, Keystone, U.S. Army)

Library of Congress Cataloging-in-Publication Data
Bodden, Valerie.
The Holocaust / by Valerie Bodden.
p. cm. – (Days of change)
Includes bibliographical references and index.
ISBN-13: 978-1-58341-547-4
1. Holocaust, Jewish (1939–1945) I. Title.
D804.3.B63 2007
940.53'18–dc22   2006019826

9 8 7 6 5 4 3 2

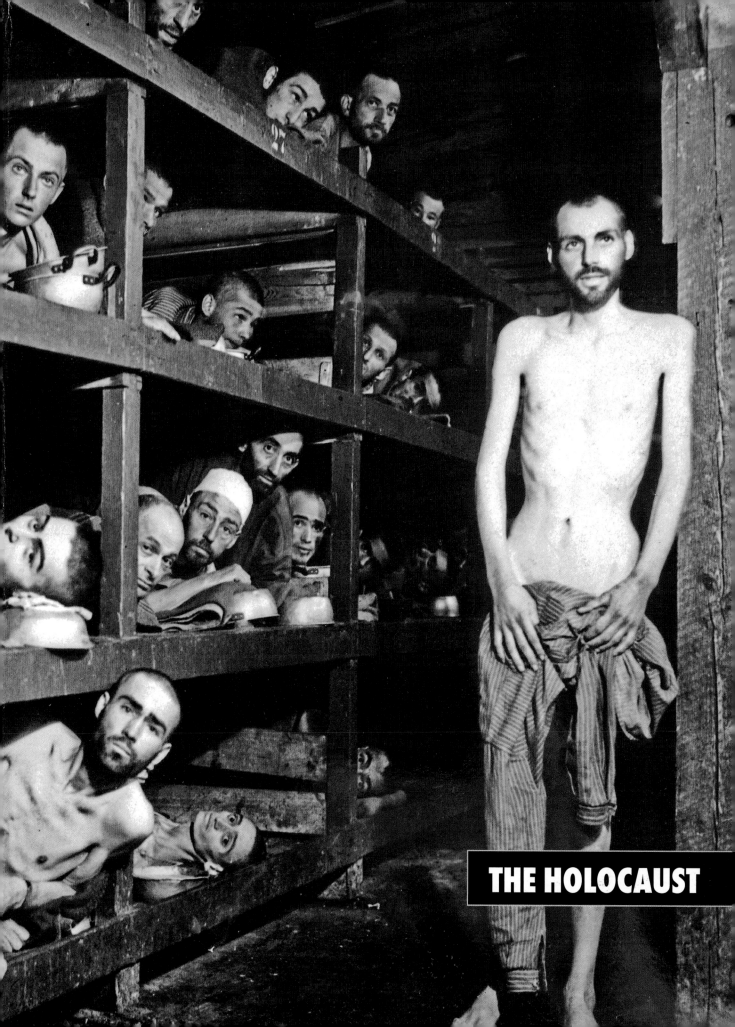

THE HOLOCAUST

At some Nazi death camps, all that remained of dead Holocaust victims were piles of used shoes; at the Majdanek, Poland, camp, more than 500,000 shoes were discovered.

Unable to believe

their eyes, horrified Soviet soldiers looked around the barbed-wire enclosed camp called Auschwitz, which they had just freed from Nazi German control. Heaps of shoes, clothing, and even bales of human hair spilled from the camp's warehouses. Even more disturbing, piles of naked, dead bodies covered the ground outside. Inside the camp's barracks were nearly 7,000 people, most of them Jewish, and all of them starving, exhausted, and barely clinging to life. Most, too weak to move, could barely comprehend—let alone celebrate—the fact that they were finally free. For them, the terrible Holocaust was over.

Unfortunately, the end of the Holocaust had come too late for more than six million Jews and five million non-Jews, who had been killed at the hands of the Nazis. For six years, from 1939 to 1945, these Holocaust victims had been shot in their villages, starved in fenced-off ghettos, or gassed en masse at death camps. Even for those who had survived, the long struggle to rebuild their lives was just beginning. Out of that struggle would come a new Jewish homeland in Palestine, as well as a dedication on the part of survivors to tell their stories, determined that never would there be another Holocaust.

5

The 1930s were a time of hardship for people around the world, who suffered from the effects of the Great Depression. This worldwide economic collapse began in the United States with the October 29, 1929, crash of the stock market (a financial exchange in which people purchase shares, or percentages, of companies). During the crash—in which the value of stocks dropped dramatically—many people lost all the money they had invested in the market. With nothing left, investors were unable to repay their bank loans, causing banks to fail and countless people to lose all their savings. Soon, the effects of the stock market crash were being felt around the world, as suddenly poor consumers were unable to purchase products, a domino effect that forced businesses to go bankrupt and left millions of people unemployed.

A WORLD IN DEPRESSION

In the U.S., where the effects of the Great Depression were first felt, more than 15 million Americans—nearly 25 percent of the country's workers—were out of work by 1933. Even those who managed to retain their jobs were often dealt sharp wage cuts, and many could find only part-time employment. Without money to pay the mortgages on their homes, thousands of people soon found themselves in shantytowns, living in crude shelters constructed of old crates and scrap metal.

Everywhere in the country, food supplies became scarce, and many families went hungry. The most desperate picked weeds or searched landfills for their next meal. Adding to the misery, a severe drought

6

During the Great Depression, American soup kitchens were faced with huge numbers of people in need, many of whom were willing to wait in long lines for a bite to eat.

turned topsoil on farms in the middle of the nation to dust, which was easily blown away on the wind, leaving thousands of small farmers without a livelihood. Even after President Franklin Roosevelt began a massive recovery program known as the New Deal, which included large public works projects employing thousands of jobless Americans, many in the nation continued to struggle. By the end of the 1930s, about 15 percent of Americans remained unemployed.

To the south of the U.S., the countries of Central and South America were also hard-hit by the Depression, which created not only financial hardship but also political upheaval in many areas. In Guatemala, declining exports in coffee and bananas gave rise to a repressive military government. Farther south, in Chile, the falling prices of the country's exports led to increased discontent with dictator Carlos Ibáñez del Campo, and workers began to strike, calling for his resignation. Unable to deal with the crisis, del Campo relinquished his post in 1931, leaving the country in chaos.

Across the world, in the Far East as well, the Depression brought not only unemployment and financial distress, but also conflict, as worker layoffs and financial difficulties were blamed on the government. In 1931, the Japanese military occupied Manchuria in northeastern China, seeking to control resource-rich regions that would provide land for

The Works Progress Administration, set up in 1935 to provide jobs for the unemployed, was part of America's New Deal and until 1943 was the largest employer in the U.S.

A crowd in Tokyo, Japan, welcomes home soldiers after their successful invasion of Manchuria in 1931; Japan, like Germany later in the decade, sought more "living space."

farming and metals such as iron ore for use in Japanese industries. Soon, Japan began to build up its military in preparation for further expansion into Southeast Asia, which would eventually lead to the country's involvement in World War II.

Northwest of Japan, in the Soviet Union, a new Communist regime had recently taken over. Under the leadership of dictator Joseph Stalin, the government worked to rapidly industrialize the nation and create large collective farms, on which farmers were forced to work for the government. Although the result of these reforms was a strong economy, large segments of the population were left living in misery, and those who disagreed with Communist rule were often jailed or executed.

Meanwhile, in the industrialized nations of Europe, the Depression hit hard. Even before the 1930s,

After dictator Joseph Stalin assumed power in the 1920s, the Soviet Union was forcibly transformed from a peasant society to an industrial power within a decade.

poverty had been widespread in Britain, and with the onset of the Depression, unemployment quickly rose to two and a half million. In an effort to increase the profitability of British businesses, people were encouraged to buy British cars and other products, and government programs to build houses were begun.

In Germany, the effects of the Depression were even more devastating, as the country, which had been defeated in World War I a decade before, was still strug-gling to pay reparations (money demanded by the victors in a war) to the U.S., Britain, France, and other Allied nations. By the end of 1932, 40 percent of Germans were out of work, and many were forced to stand in long lines for food rations. German money became almost worthless, with so little value that parents allowed their children to use stacks of it as toy bricks.

As the German people struggled to survive from day to day, many recalled the glory days before World War I, when their country had been an industrial power to be reckoned with, as well as a center of European arts and culture. Amid this environment of hardship and growing discontent arose a new, strong voice, promising to provide Germany's citizens a better life and to establish a new

"It is the silence that frightens me so in the evenings and at night. . . . I can't tell you how oppressive it is never to be able to go outdoors; also I'm very afraid that we shall be discovered and be shot. . . . We have to whisper and tread lightly during the day; otherwise the people in the warehouse might hear us."

ANNE FRANK, diary entry while in hiding during the Holocaust, July 11, 1942

12

By 1923, German money was worth one million times less than it had been worth before
World War I, making banknotes more useful as toys than as money.

"I believed the propaganda that all Jews were criminals and subhumans and that they were the cause of Germany's decline after the First World War. The thought that one should disobey or evade the order to participate in the extermination of the Jews did not therefore enter my mind at all."

KURT MÖBIUS, former German police officer who served at the Chelmno, Poland, extermination camp, 1961

German dictator Adolf Hitler

Germany, more glorious than ever. The voice belonged to Adolf Hitler, the leader of the National Socialist German Workers Party, or Nazis, and people across the country rallied around it. In 1932, the Nazis were elected the largest party in parliament, and the next year, German President Paul von Hindenburg appointed Hitler chancellor. When Hindenburg died in 1934, Hitler gave himself a new title: Führer, or sole leader, of Germany.

Almost immediately after coming to power, Hitler began to build up the German army. At the same time, he set in motion a program to create a "pure" Germany made up of only Aryans—white, blue-eyed, Germanic people, whom Hitler considered the ideal race. In order to purge the country of "defects," Hitler required the forced sterilization of Germany's mentally and physically handicapped (eventually, many would be put to death in "mercy killings"), as well as of Roma people (sometimes called Gypsies).

Hitler's main focus in purifying Germany, however, was to make the country *Judenrein*, or cleansed of Jews. Although less than one percent of the country's population of 64 million was Jewish, Hitler claimed that Jews had caused all of Germany's problems. Viewing Jews not as followers of a specific religion but as a separate race, Hitler

15

Throughout much of the 1930s, the Nazis held huge propaganda rallies in Nuremberg, Germany, at which Adolf Hitler was glorified and the Jews vilified.

quickly established laws aimed at making life so miserable for Jewish people that they would have no choice but to leave the country. Soon, signs proclaiming "Jews prohibited" were posted in stores, restaurants, and other businesses throughout Germany. In 1935, a new set of laws, known as the Nuremberg Laws, took away the citizenship rights of Jews in Germany, who were no longer allowed to vote or to marry other Germans.

The full force of German anger against the Jews was unleashed on the night of November 9, 1938, as anti-Jewish violence erupted across Germany and Austria (which had been annexed to Germany a few months before). For two days, Jewish properties were trashed, looted, and burned by Nazis and German citizens in what would come to be known as *Kristallnacht*, or the "Night of Broken Glass." When the violence ended, more than 1,000 synagogues and 7,000 Jewish businesses were severely damaged or destroyed, and more than 90 Jews were dead. The next morning, 30,000 Jewish men were rounded up and taken to concentration camps, which had been set up to hold "enemies" of the Nazis, including Communists, Jehovah's Witnesses (members of a religious group who refuse to show allegiance to any government),

"And we say that the war will not end as the Jews imagine it will, . . . but the result of this war will be the complete annihilation of the Jews. And the further this war spreads, the further will spread this fight against the world of the [Jew], and they will be used as food for every prison camp. . . . The hour will come when the enemy of all times, or at least of the last thousand years, will have played his part to the end."

ADOLF HITLER, German dictator, January 30, 1942

Adolf Hitler was born in Austria, where his anti-Semitic (or anti-Jewish) feelings developed early, influenced by the claims of Viennese mayor Karl Lueger that Jews were responsible for hard economic times. In 1913, Hitler moved to Germany, where he enlisted in the army and served in World War I. After the war, Hitler joined the Nazi party and soon rose to the top of its ranks. Although he had little formal education—he didn't complete high school—Hitler was able to play upon the concerns of his countrymen, and his spellbinding speeches, in which he called Jews "the personification of the devil," soon earned him a wide following.

Under Hitler's rule, anti-Semitism was given free rein, leading to the events of Kristallnacht, after which Germany charged the Jews $400 million for damages.

Before the Holocaust, Jews lived in every country of Europe. The largest populations were located in eastern Europe, with 3.25 million Jews in Poland alone. Eastern European Jews often lived in separate Jewish towns called *shtetls*, where most spoke Yiddish (a combination of German and Hebrew) and observed traditional Jewish customs. In the larger cities of eastern Europe, as well as in the countries of western Europe, including Germany, France, and Belgium, most Jews adopted the culture and language of the larger population. Many were well-educated, serving as accountants, doctors, and professors at some of their countries' finest universities.

As anti-Jewish sentiment increased in the years leading up to World War II, thousands of Polish Jews were expelled from Germany and forced to live in stables and huts.

Roma, homosexuals, and now Jews.

In the months that followed Kristallnacht, many Jews who had not already fled Germany searched for ways out of the country. The 350,000 who remained were listed in the Germans' Jewish Registry, which contained information about all of the Jews living in German-controlled territory. Less than a year after Kristallnacht, on September 1, 1939, the Germans— seeking to gain living space for their "perfect" race—invaded Poland, setting off World War II. At the same time, their war against the Jews and other German "enemies" began to intensify.

With the outbreak of World War II, the Great Depression effectively came to an end, as the nations of Europe—soon to be joined by the U.S.—geared up for war, employing millions in their war industries and pouring massive sums of money into their militaries. Despite such preparations, however, by 1940 the Germans had defeated Poland, France, Belgium, Luxembourg, Holland, Denmark, and Norway, bringing an additional 90 million people, and nearly four million Jews, under Hitler's control.

Soon, Jews almost everywhere in the Reich, or German Empire, were forced to wear identifying marks, such as a yellow Star of David, on their clothing. In countries such as Austria and Poland, where anti-Semitism, or hatred of Jews, had already been strong before Germany's invasion, Jews were often forced to perform humiliating tasks, such as cleaning the streets with toothbrushes.

The Nazis weren't satisfied with simply mistreating Jews, however. Near the end of 1939, they began to order Jews, as well as many Roma people, into marked-off—and

THE "FINAL SOLUTION"

usually walled- or fenced-off—areas of various cities. These areas, known as ghettos, were often in the most run-down sections of cities and soon became overcrowded. In the largest ghetto, established in Warsaw, Poland, more than 400,000 people were packed into a 100-block area, requiring several families to cram into one small apartment. Thousands who couldn't find a home lived on the streets, where

One of the heroes of the Warsaw ghetto was Janusz Korczak, a Jewish doctor who had been ordered to look after the children of the ghetto's orphanage. Korczak embraced his new role, treating the orphans as his own children. When the Nazis informed Korczak that he would be allowed to stay in the ghetto but his 192 children would be deported, he convinced the guards to allow him to remain with the children. He calmly went with the orphans to the Treblinka extermination camp, where he entered the gas chambers with them, telling them stories and urging them to be brave even in their last moments.

Dead bodies in the street quickly became a common site in the Warsaw ghetto; despite such horrors, parents tried to make life as normal as possible for their children.

many froze to death. Others died of starvation, deliberately inflicted by the Germans, who permitted ghetto residents to buy only a small amount of bread, potatoes, and fat. Many fell victim to contagious diseases such as typhus, which spread rapidly in the unsanitary conditions of the ghetto.

Even those ghetto residents who managed to avoid disease and starvation often found themselves helpless victims of random acts of Nazi violence. In the Warsaw ghetto, one guard took pleasure in walking through the streets and shooting babies in strollers. Others enjoyed driving their trucks at high speeds into crowds of Jewish ghetto residents. The unarmed Jews could do little to protect themselves from such acts of cruelty.

While thousands of Jews were being killed in the ghettos, Jews, along with Roma and Communists,

Although some Jews escaped during the Warsaw ghetto uprising of 1943, 50,000 were rounded up and deported to extermination camps after the revolt was put down.

Countless Holocaust victims were buried in mass graves, some dug with their own hands;
this man kneels at the edge of an open grave and waits for a Nazi soldier to kill him.

were being executed in their hometowns in the Soviet Union and Eastern Europe. After the Germans invaded the Soviet Union in June 1941, special Nazi squads known as *Einsatzgruppen* marched the Jewish populations of entire towns to open fields, where they forced the Jews to undress and stand in front of huge ditches that had been dug in the ground. The Jews were then shot, falling conveniently into the mass graves.

Yet the Nazis were still not satisfied with the progress in their quest to make the Reich Judenrein. On January 20, 1942, Nazi leaders met in the neighborhood of Wannsee in Berlin to discuss the "Final Solution" to the Jewish "problem." By "Final Solution," they meant the systematic murder of all of Europe and the Soviet Union's 11 million Jews. Immediately after their meeting, the Nazis informed the Jews in the ghettos that they were to be "resettled." They also began to round up Jews throughout Europe who hadn't been deported to the ghettos. Realizing that their best chance of survival was to evade the Nazis, many Jews quickly went into hiding, seeking refuge in stables, attics, caverns, and even closets.

Most of those Jews who remained unhidden were herded

"We were assembled in a field in Bielsko [a ghetto in Poland]. After about four hours, the SS men [Nazi guards] finally came in a shiny black car, with their shiny boots. They checked lists. We were all there. Why did we all walk meek like sheep to the slaughterhouse? Why did we not fight back, run, hide? Because we did not think that human beings were able to commit the crimes that were being committed."

GERDA WEISSMANN, Holocaust survivor, 1957

25

onto trains, 100 or more to a box-car, their bodies packed so closely together that there was no room to move. For anywhere from a few hours to a few days, they remained in the cars, which had no seats or bathrooms and only slats in the wall for windows. Many, especially the old, young, and sick, died along the way. When the trains finally stopped, those who had survived the harsh conditions were often relieved, thinking that the worst was over. They were sadly mistaken.

The destination for most of the trains was one of six Nazi extermination, or death, camps in Poland. The largest of these was Auschwitz-Birkenau, which also served as a labor camp. Prisoners disembarking from the trains there were "sorted" by a Nazi physician, who quickly looked at each person, then directed him or her to the left or right. The

Jews being "resettled" were told to bring all of their valuables with them; that way, when they reached their destination, the Nazis could plunder their belongings.

Jews were promptly divided by Nazi officials after arriving at camps; many Jews, relieved to be off the trains, thought they would face merely forced labor at the camps.

group formed to the left consisted mainly of children, pregnant women, the elderly, the handicapped, and the sick. The group on the right was made up of able-bodied adults and healthy teenagers.

Those in the group to the left were immediately sent to large "shower rooms," where they were told to undress. Once they were all inside, guards locked the shower room doors and, instead of turning on the water, released Zyklon B, a toxic insecticide, into the room. After 10 to 15 panic-filled minutes, everyone in the gas chamber—often up to 2,000 people— was dead from lack of oxygen. Prisoners from the camp were then forced to pull the bodies from the room, remove the hair (to be sold for use in making ropes, mattresses, and other products), gold teeth, and fillings from them, and burn them in large crematoria, or ovens designed to burn human bodies.

"The shaving off of our hair was the most traumatic experience. It made me feel utterly vulnerable and reduced to a complete nobody. I had relinquished my clothes as well, and I stood there stark naked, bald, and with a number on my arm. In the space of a few minutes, I had been stripped of every vestige of human dignity and become indistinguishable from everyone around me."

ANITA LASKER-WALLFISCH, Holocaust survivor, 1996

29

Meanwhile, those who had been sent to the right as they exited the train were taken to have their heads shaved and a number—their new form of identification—tattooed on their arms. They were stripped of their clothes and given ragged, ill-fitting clothing and mismatched shoes. Then they were sent to cold, windowless barracks, where eight peo-

Conditions in the Nazi concentration camps were so brutal that a system of "each man for himself" often developed. In order to survive, those imprisoned could have regard for no one but themselves, not even their family. Lee Potasinski, a survivor of Auschwitz, recalled seeing a sick father sitting next to his son, who was eating a raw potato. When the father asked for a piece of the potato, his son said, "No, I can't." Potasinski remembered thinking at the time that the son's response made complete sense: "When it came to food," he said, "there was no such thing as sharing."

One of Germany's earliest concentration camps, at Oranienburg, housed mostly communists and social democrats, who were forced to perform hard labor.

ple crowded together on each shelf of the wooden bunks that lined the room. For the remainder of their time at Auschwitz, the prisoners were forced to work 12 hours or more a day, with little food to sustain them. They were beaten for the slightest provocation—or for no reason at all. Most survived only a few months. When they died, they were replaced by the prisoners—mostly Jews, but also Roma, non-Jewish Poles, and others—on the trains that kept rolling into camp.

Trains also continued to roll into the other five Nazi extermination camps (at Chelmno, Treblinka, Sobibór, Belzec, and Majdanek-Lublin), where prospects for survival were even worse than at Auschwitz. Since most of these camps were designed exclusively as killing centers, the Germans had no need for live prisoners, and the new arrivals at most were taken immediately to be gassed. Only a few were spared for the grisly task of burying or burning the bodies.

In addition to their six extermination camps, the Nazis also set up a number of camps throughout Germany, Austria, Yugoslavia, and France intended to function solely as labor camps for Jews, Roma, communists, homosexuals, and others the Germans considered inferior or dangerous. Although

"It was early evening when the train stopped and the doors opened. As I came off the train, I saw on the left huge chimneys belching forth thick, black smoke. There was a strange smell, like burning the feathers off a chicken before it was cooked. I didn't know that the smoke and the smell were not from chickens. I didn't know, until I found out later on, that I was smelling our own flesh, our own families burning."

ERNEST HONIG, Holocaust survivor at Auschwitz, 1989

31

not equipped with gas chambers, these camps were still deadly. On an average day, 15 to 40 of every 100 people in the labor camps died, victims of overwork, starvation, disease, and Nazi brutality. As at Auschwitz, prisoners were often forced to work 12 hours a day, some at factories making goods to support the German war effort, others at senseless jobs—such as running up quarry steps while carrying a huge rock—created simply to torment them.

Many of the Nazi concentration camps continued to operate at full power until 1944. But on July 23 of that year, the Soviets liberated Poland's Majdanek extermination camp. By the winter, the Germans, realizing that Allied (American, British, French, and Soviet) troops were closing in, began to send prisoners—first by train and then by foot—from camps throughout Europe to camps inside Germany. Many were shot along the way, earning these forced marches the name "death marches." Those who survived the marches were crowded into already overfilled camps, where the death totals continued to rise. Over the next 10 months, Allied troops liberated these camps as well, horrified each time by the evidence of the terrible acts that had been committed within them.

"For the great part of the liberated Jews . . . there was no ecstasy, no joy at our liberation. We had lost our families, our homes. We had no place to go, nobody to hug, nobody who was waiting for us, anywhere. We had been liberated from death and the fear of death, but we were not free from the fear of life."

HADASSAH BIMKO ROSENSAFT, Holocaust survivor at Bergen-Belsen concentration camp, 1994

When American troops entered Dachau concentration camp, they found 32,000 inmates—weakened but still alive—along with hundreds of dead bodies.

World War II in Europe ended with Germany's surrender on May 7, 1945. By that time, news of the Nazi slaughter of the Jews and others had reached the rest of the world. Photos of victims were plastered on the pages of newspapers and magazines and filled newsreels. Yet, for thousands of Holocaust victims, the horror wasn't over. In the days and weeks after the liberation of labor and extermination

NEVER AGAIN

camps, thousands continued to die of disease and starvation—for many, the food offered by the liberating troops was too much for their weakened bodies to handle, and they died after eating it.

Even for those who survived after liberation, life seemed hopeless. Many tried to pick up the pieces of their lives but soon discovered that there were no pieces to pick up.

Their families and friends—in some cases, their entire communities—had been wiped out. Many found their homes destroyed, and even those that remained standing were often occupied by strangers who were unwilling to give them back. Worst of all, many Jews who tried to return to their homes became victims of violence once again, as the end of the Holocaust had not brought with it the end of anti-Semitic feelings, especially in eastern Europe. In Poland, in the first seven months after the war, more than 500 Jews who returned to their homes were killed.

With nowhere else to turn, many survivors fled to displaced persons camps, which had been set up by the Allies at the sites of former concentration camps in western Europe to shelter the more than 10 million

By the time they were liberated from Nazi concentration camps, most Jews were shadows of their former selves, having lost 50 to 60 percent of their body weight.

Some of the information about the Holocaust that exists today comes from the diaries of victims, many of them children. Perhaps the most famous account of the Holocaust comes from a young Jewish girl named Anne Frank, whose family hid in a small attic above a warehouse in the Netherlands beginning in 1942. The Frank family was discovered in 1944, and Anne was eventually sent to Bergen-Belsen concentration camp, where she died, one of more than one and a half million child victims of the Holocaust. Anne's father survived the war and later had her diary published as a witness to the Holocaust.

Only 11 percent of Jewish children survived the Holocaust, most because they had gone into hiding, although some, like this boy, managed to survive the concentration camps.

people across the continent who had been left homeless by the war. Life in the displaced persons camps was little better for Holocaust victims than it had been under Nazi rule. In some cases, survivors were stuck wearing their old concentration camp uniforms or the uniforms of Nazi guards, and they often found themselves living in the same quarters as their former camp guards. By the fall of 1945, however, condi-tions in the camps had improved, as had conditions in the rest of Europe, to which many survivors finally returned. Others settled overseas in the U.S., which took in 400,000 European refugees, about a third of them Jewish, in the first few years after the war.

But thousands of Jews still remained without a home, and many campaigned for the creation of a Jewish state in the Middle Eastern

After the war, many Jewish refugees in Germany lived off meager rations of bread—one loaf for every four people each day—while they searched for a new land to call home.

land of Palestine, which for thousands of years the Jews had considered their homeland, promised to them by God. Their dream was finally realized on May 14, 1948, with the United Nations-backed formation of the state of Israel. Yet the establishment of a Jewish homeland did not necessarily mean peace for the thousands of Jews who flocked to Israel, as Arab Palestinians—out of whose lands Israel had been carved—and Jewish Israelis immediately began to fight over territory. Even today, nearly 60 years later, violence between Arabs and Jews continues to rock the region.

While survivors of the Holocaust were slowly working to rebuild their lives in the immediate aftermath of World War II, the Allies were trying to determine how to best bring to justice those who had been responsible for the systematic murder of 11

The UN, set up after World War II to support global peace, was quick to act after the Holocaust to protect the human rights of future generations. In 1948, the organization made the mass murder, or genocide, of particular peoples an international crime. That same year, the UN published the Universal Declaration of Human Rights, which outlines the rights of all people, including the rights to life, liberty, and security of person. Despite these measures, genocide has not come to an end; as recently as 1994, large-scale genocide was carried out in the African nation of Rwanda.

Even before the creation of the nation of Israel, many Jewish survivors of the Holocaust tried to flee to Palestine, although large numbers were turned back as illegal immigrants.

Despite the fact that evidence of the Holocaust abounds, some today deny that it occurred. Holocaust denial began in the mid-1960s and gained popularity in 1977, when American professor Arthur Butz published a book in which he denounced the Holocaust as a hoax. Some deniers today claim that the Holocaust is a Jewish ploy designed to validate Israel's existence or to extract money from Germany. Others deny aspects of the Holocaust, saying that Jews perished but not on the scale reported and not in the gas chambers, but from the effects of war. Today, Holocaust denial is illegal in Germany and can lead to fines and prison terms.

In sentencing Hermann Göring to death, the International Military Tribunal stated that his "own admissions [were] more than sufficiently wide to be conclusive of his guilt."

million people. In August 1945, the Allies decided to try 22 Nazi leaders—which did not include Hitler, who had killed himself in the last days of the war—before an International Military Tribunal made up of Allied judges. The defendants were charged with conspiracy, crimes against peace, war crimes, and crimes against humanity.

At the trials, which were held in Nuremberg, Germany, films that had been taken of the concentration camps shortly after the Allies arrived stunned those who watched, as did physical evidence, such as a large piece of tattooed skin that had been used as a lampshade. But most damaging to the Nazis were the extensive records they had kept with their own hands, detailing the names, dates of arrival, and dates and causes of death of thousands of prisoners (although no record was kept of those who were gassed immediately). Few of the Nazis on trial denied that they had participated in the Holocaust; instead, most insisted that they were not guilty because they had simply been following orders. The judges disagreed. On September 30, 1946, 19 of the 22 Nazi defendants were found guilty. Twelve of them—including Hermann Göring, once Hitler's designated succes-

"And we were just sitting there talking, and the only thing that we were saying to each other was, if we ever get out alive, there were two things that we would like to do. One is to be able to have enough food to eat—and we thought that that would never happen again. And number two, to be able to tell others of what happened. Although we were sure at that time—and we said to each other—that nobody's going to believe us."

LEE POTASINSKI, Holocaust survivor at Auschwitz and Dachau concentration camps, 1998

41

sor, and Nazi racial theorist Alfred Rosenberg—were sentenced to death by hanging (although Göring committed suicide the night before his scheduled execution).

For years after the Nuremberg Trials, trials of Nazi criminals continued to be held in several countries. In the five years following the war, Allied and German courts (which were no longer under Nazi control) tried almost 10,000 people for war crimes. Israel sought prosecution of Nazi leaders into the 1980s, although its greatest success came in 1962 with the capture, trial, and execution of Adolf Eichmann, the leader of the Nazi extermination program. Even today, elderly Nazi criminals are occasionally found in hiding and brought to trial in various countries.

In the years since the Holocaust, Germany has struggled to come to grips with the atrocities that were committed in its name. Since the 1950s, the country has paid $93 billion to Holocaust survivors and to Israel. Germany acknowledges that these payments in no way lessen the country's guilt in the Holocaust; instead, they are partial compensation for survivors' lost income and stolen property.

Many today insist, however, that it isn't only Germany that bears guilt for the Holocaust. They place some of the blame on the millions of people in Nazi-occupied Europe who knew what was happening and stood idly by. Indeed, many individuals, frightened of the Nazis or prejudiced against the Jews, watched silently as their neighbors were deported. Even powerful groups that learned of Nazi atrocities, including the Catholic Church, refused to speak out. In 1942, the

During his trial, which was broadcast live around the world, Adolf Eichmann sat behind bulletproof glass as nearly 100 Holocaust survivors testified against him.

"Never before in
human history
had a state and a
political movement
dedicated itself to
the destruction of
a whole people.
. . . In every case
of terrible human
destructiveness
that we have
known, . . . killing
was not an end in
itself, but a means
to an end. . . .
[But] the German
dictatorship
murdered the
Jews for the sake
of murdering the
Jews. For the
Germans [took]
to themselves the
decision as to who
was entitled to live
on this Earth and
who was not. That
is the uniqueness
of the Holocaust."

LUCY S. DAWIDOWICZ,
American historian,
1977

U.S. learned of the Nazi plan to exterminate Jews. Yet, insisting that the best way to solve the problem was to concentrate on bringing the Germans to quick defeat, the U.S. took no direct action to rescue Jews until 1944, when it allowed about 1,000 Jewish refugees from southern Italy to enter the country.

Rather than directing criticism or placing blame, some people have chosen instead to focus on the thousands of individuals who risked their lives to save their friends, neighbors, and strangers. In Israel, the Holocaust museum Yad Vashem strives not only to preserve the memories of those who died in the Holocaust, but also to honor the "righteous Gentiles," or non-Jews, who helped save the lives of countless Jews during the Holocaust. Today, more than 21,300 righteous Gentiles have been recognized, among them Oskar Schindler, a factory owner in Poland who saved more than 1,000 Jews who worked for him by convincing Nazi officials to allow him to relocate his plant—along with his employees, who were slated to be deported to extermination camps—to Czechoslovakia.

Other Holocaust memorials and museums around the world also pay tribute to both the heroes and victims of the

"I have not got over my guilt that I am alive, and I think many of us have that problem. Rationally, I know that it is not my fault that I survived, but guilt is not always a rational thing. . . . It is a difficult thing to live with. I can't explain my guilt, but I am always conscious of it. I have tried to [get rid of] it in my work [as a rabbi], but I don't succeed."

HUGO GRYN, Holocaust survivor, 1988

Oskar Schindler (waving) was received as a hero in Israel; when he died in Germany in 1974, those he had helped to save brought his body to Israel to be buried.

Although many countries conquered by Nazi Germany stood by as their Jewish population was deported to ghettos and concentration camps, Denmark did all it could to save its Jewish citizens. When a sympathetic Nazi leader managed to get word to Danish authorities that raids of the country's Jewish communities would soon take place, the Danes organized a nationwide campaign to slip Jews out of Denmark. With the help of thousands of Danish citizens, 7,200 of Denmark's 8,000 Jews were transported to neutral Sweden. Although 500 of the Jews who didn't escape were deported to a ghetto in Czechoslovakia, only 51 died, thanks largely to pressure by Danish officials.

Today, people from around the world visit the museum at Auschwitz, where victims' photographs hang as silent witnesses of the atrocities committed during the Holocaust.

Holocaust. Many former concentration camps, including Auschwitz, have become museums dedicated to the memory of the millions who perished on their lands. At some, survivors, now in old age, conduct tours, recounting the atrocities they experienced. Over the years, other survivors have written books about their treatment during the Holocaust. Others simply speak—to their family, their friends, or school-children—of the unimaginable suffering they endured and the guilt they felt at having survived when so many of their loved ones perished. These survivors share their painful memories with one overriding hope: that in telling of their past, they can prevent it from becoming another's future.

BIBLIOGRAPHY

Adler, David. *We Remember the Holocaust.*
New York: Henry Holt and Company, 1989.

Altman, Linda Jacobs. *Impact of the Holocaust.*
Berkeley Heights, N.J.: Enslow, 2004.

Ayer, Eleanor, and Stephen Chicoine. *From the Ashes.*
Woodbridge, Conn.: Blackbirch Press, 1998.

Bachrach, Susan. *Tell Them We Remember: The Story of the Holocaust.*
New York: Little, Brown and Company, 1994.

Rogasky, Barbara. *Smoke and Ashes: The Story of the Holocaust.*
New York: Holiday House, 2002.

Saldinger, Anne Grenn. *Life in a Nazi Concentration Camp.*
San Diego: Lucent, 2001.

Stewart, Gail. *Life in the Warsaw Ghetto.*
San Diego: Lucent, 1995.

INDEX